Carolin Schirmer

30 Mini-Bücher für den Englischunterricht

Erste Texte mit kurzen Arbeitsaufträgen

Verlag an der Ruhr

Impressum

Titel
30 Mini-Bücher für den Englischunterricht
Erste Texte mit kurzen Arbeitsaufträgen

Autorin
Carolin Schirmer

Umschlagmotiv
Verlag an der Ruhr, inkl. Abbildungen von Norbert Höveler

Druck
Heenemann GmbH & Co. KG, Berlin, DE

Verlag an der Ruhr
Mülheim an der Ruhr
www.verlagruhr.de

Geeignet für die Klassen 3–6

ISBN 978-3-8346-4277-6

Inhaltsverzeichnis

Titel	**Thema**	**Schwierigkeitsgrad**
Nelly's family	*family*	leicht
Benny is crazy	*food*	leicht
Happy Halloween!	*Halloween*	leicht
My Tuesday	*daily routine*	leicht
The number rhyme	*numbers*	leicht
What's missing?	*body parts, animals*	leicht
My favourite colour	*colours, animals*	leicht
Nice to meet you!	*greeting and introducing*	leicht
How are you?	*feelings*	leicht
Who am I?	*vehicles*	leicht
Let's have breakfast!	*breakfast*	mittel
Bad weather	*weather*	mittel
Greg's week	*days of the week, hobbies*	mittel
New clothes for Jenna	*clothes*	mittel
Freddy's year	*seasons*	mittel
Merry Christmas	*Christmas*	mittel
Oh no, Tiffy!	*rooms*	mittel
Nicky can do it better	*hobbies, comparisons*	mittel
Let's go to school	*directions*	mittel
Busy day	*household*	mittel
Opposites	*adjectives, animals*	mittel
Lilly's birthday	*birthday*	mittel
Fruit rhyme	*fruits, like and dislike*	mittel
At the bakery	*shopping, bakery products*	mittel
A toy for Anna	*toys, like and dislike*	mittel
I spy with my little eye …	*colours*	schwierig
Phil goes to school	*school, school things*	schwierig
Pets	*pets*	schwierig
Suri in London	*London/Great Britain*	schwierig
The Valentine's card	*Valentine's day*	schwierig

Vorwort

Liebe Lehrer*innen,

wenn man in Ihrer Klasse eine Umfrage zu den Lieblingsfächern der Kinder starten würde, kämen sicherlich ganz unterschiedliche Ergebnisse heraus. Jedes Kind kann sich für unterschiedliche Fächer besonders begeistern. Als Englischlehrkräfte kennen Sie aber sicher das Phänomen: Das Fach Englisch ist für die meisten Kinder besonders motivierend. Für einen Großteil der Kinder ist Englisch die erste Fremdsprache und dementsprechend etwas Besonderes. Voller Begeisterung und Stolz sprechen die Schüler*innen immer wieder die neu erlernten Wörter und Sätze, lauschen Hörtexten oder singen englische Lieder.

Lesen und Schreiben nehmen dagegen gerade zu Beginn des Englischlernens oft noch einen geringen Stellenwert ein, wenngleich das Schriftbild die Schüler*innen bei der Verankerung des Gelernten durchaus unterstützen kann. An dieser Stelle setzen die Mini-Bücher an, die Sie gerade in den Händen halten.

Die insgesamt 30 Mini-Bücher, die Sie in diesem Heft als Kopiervorlagen finden, werden von den Kindern selbst gefaltet, gelesen und mitgestaltet. Jede Kopiervorlage enthält dabei eine kurze Geschichte in einfachem Englisch, die bereits für Kinder ab der 3. Klasse verständlich ist. Die zu den Geschichten passenden Illustrationen auf jeder Seite erleichtern den Kindern dabei zusätzlich das Verständnis und eignen sich außerdem zum Ausmalen.

Zusätzlich zu den Geschichten finden sich auf den letzten beiden Seiten der Mini-Bücher stets einfache, auf die Geschichte abgestimmte Arbeitsaufträge, bei denen die Schüler*innen bekanntes Wortmaterial schreiben, Bilder malen oder richtige Antworten suchen müssen.

Die Mini-Bücher helfen den Kindern spielerisch dabei, ihren Wortschatz zu erweitern, und sorgen für eine zusätzliche Portion Motivation im Englischunterricht: Ein „eigenes“, kleines Buch zu haben, das man selbst mitgestaltet, ist für die Kinder etwas ganz Besonderes. Die Bücher werden zu Sammelobjekten, die immer wieder gern (vor-)gelesen und auch den Eltern zu Hause gezeigt werden.

Und ob Sie die Mini-Bücher als Einstiegsritual in ein neues Thema, als Abwechslung in einer Vertretungsstunde oder einfach zwischendurch nutzen wollen, bleibt ganz Ihnen überlassen.

Ich wünsche Ihnen und Ihren Schüler*innen auf jeden Fall viel Spaß beim Lesen, Gestalten, Schreiben und Entdecken!

Herzlichst
Carolin Schirmer

Der Verlag an der Ruhr legt großen Wert auf eine geschlechtergerechte und inklusive Sprache. Daher nutzen wir bevorzugt das Gendersternchen, um sowohl männliche und weibliche als auch nichtbinäre Geschlechtsidentitäten einzuschließen. Alternativ verwenden wir neutrale Formulierungen.

Zum Einsatz im Unterricht

Um die Mini-Bücher optimal in Ihren Unterricht zu integrieren, finden Sie im Folgenden ein paar Tipps.

- Die Mini-Bücher können, je nach Lernstand, von den Kindern **selbstständig bearbeitet** werden. Auch wenn noch nicht jedes einzelne Wort bekannt sein sollte, gelingt es den Kindern zumeist, über den Kontext sowie die passenden Bilder den Inhalt der Geschichte zu erschließen.
  Bei den Arbeitsaufträgen handelt es sich wiederum um **einfache Arbeitsanweisungen**, bei denen oft auch schon ein erster Lösungsschritt vorgegeben ist, um das Verständnis zu erleichtern.
  Sollte eine Geschichte noch sehr viel unbekanntes Wortmaterial enthalten, empfiehlt es sich ggf., entweder vorher das benötigte Vokabular explizit einzuführen oder das Mini-Buch einmal im Plenum zu besprechen.

- Die Mini-Bücher werden alle nach dem gleichen, einfach verständlichen Prinzip gefaltet. Wenn die Schüler*innen dieses Prinzip einmal verstanden haben, lässt es sich also für alle Mini-Bücher genau so einsetzen. Hierzu ist es wichtig, die **Faltanleitung** einmal mit der ganzen Klasse zu besprechen und ein Mini-Buch exemplarisch zu falten.
  Sollte die Falttechnik bei Ihren Schüler*innen doch einmal in Vergessenheit geraten, finden Sie außerdem auf S. 7 und 8 zwei Kopiervorlagen für die Kinder, auf denen der Faltvorgang nochmals anschaulich beschrieben wird. Diese Anleitung können Sie als Erinnerung in der Klasse auslegen oder aufhängen, falls die Kinder des Öfteren auch selbstständig mit den Mini-Büchern arbeiten.
  Die Anleitung ist auf Deutsch verfügbar. Grundsätzlich sollte zwar bereits im frühen Englischunterricht Englisch die vorherrschende Sprache sein, allerdings ist das sehr spezielle Vokabular einer Faltanleitung für die Kinder in Schriftform meist nicht gut verständlich. Aus diesem Grund wird für die Anleitung eine deutschsprachige Version bereitgestellt.

- Das Material kann vielfältig eingesetzt werden. Wie bereits erwähnt, ist es grundsätzlich möglich, dass die Kinder die Mini-Bücher selbstständig bearbeiten. So können Sie z. B. einige Mini-Bücher als Kopiervorlagen immer in der Klasse bereitstellen, damit die Kinder sie in Freiarbeitsphasen nutzen können. Viele Kinder greifen gern darauf zurück, weil die Beschäftigung mit den Mini-Büchern für sie eine willkommene Abwechslung zu den „klassischen" Schulbuchaufgaben ist.
  Da die Mini-Bücher zu verschiedenen, gängigen Themen des Englischunterrichts passen, können Sie auch sehr gut zur Einführung oder zum Abschluss eines (neuen) Themenbereichs genutzt werden. Um die Mini-Bücher passgenau einsetzen zu können, finden Sie auf S. 3 eine **Übersicht über die Mini-Bücher, die enthaltenen Themen und eine Einschätzung der Schwierigkeitsstufe**.

- Die Bücher können von den Kindern gesammelt werden – entweder in einem **extra hierfür angelegten Ordner oder einer Box**. Erfahrungsgemäß blättern viele Schüler*innen gern immer wieder in „ihren" Büchern und zeigen sie auch Mitschüler*innen, anderen Lehrkräften oder ihren Eltern. Darüber hinaus besteht die Möglichkeit, die Bücher während einer Art Museumsrundgang zu präsentieren – das ist insbesondere dann sinnvoll, wenn nicht alle Kinder das gleiche Mini-Buch gestaltet haben.

Zum Einsatz im Unterricht

- Einige Geschichten sind gut geeignet, um sie in **Rollenspielen** nachzuspielen. Hierfür können sich die Kinder in Kleingruppen zusammenfinden und mithilfe der Bücher ihre Rollen proben. Das Rollenspiel kann anschließend vor der Klasse präsentiert werden. Auch hier ist das Ganze besonders spannend, wenn von den Gruppen jeweils unterschiedliche Geschichten nachgespielt werden.

- Die Bücher variieren bzgl. des **Schwierigkeitsgrads**, um verschiedenen Lernständen gerecht zu werden. Erfahrungsgemäß läuft der Englischunterricht insbesondere an Grundschulen sehr unterschiedlich ab, sodass viele Kinder die Mini-Bücher bereits ab Klasse 3 selbstständig nutzen können, andere hiermit wiederum noch weniger vertraut sind und mehr Unterstützung benötigen. Durch verschiedene Vorerfahrungen mit dem Englischen ist auch der Lernstand an der weiterführenden Schule dementsprechend heterogen. Hier können die Mini-Bücher eine gute Unterstützung bieten.
  Dabei ist grundsätzlich zu beachten, dass einige Bücher mehr Schrift enthalten als andere. Da die Lernstände stets variieren, können Sie als Lehrkraft am besten abschätzen, welche Mini-Bücher selbstständig bearbeitet werden können, bei welchen Geschichten Ihre Schüler*innen noch Unterstützung benötigen und welche evtl. noch zu schwierig sind. Um Ihnen die Entscheidung ein wenig zu erleichtern, sind Geschichten mit mehr Text bzw. einem etwas höheren Anspruch in der **Übersicht auf S. 3** entsprechend als „schwierig“ gekennzeichnet.

- Auf der letzten Seite finden Sie eine **Blanko-Vorlage**. Mithilfe dieser können Ihre Schüler*innen eigene Mini-Bücher erstellen. Hierbei geht es weniger darum, komplexe und grammatikalisch korrekte Texte zu schreiben, sondern darum, Spaß an der Sprache zu entwickeln. Ermutigen Sie die Kinder zum Schreiben erster Wörter. Leistungsstärkere Kinder können auch schon kurze, bekannte Sätze schreiben. Unbekanntes Vokabular kann durch das Zeichnen von Symbolen oder kleinen Bildern ersetzt werden. Viele Schüler*innen sind aber auch motiviert, schon richtige, kurze Texte zu schreiben, und können durch ein englisches Wörterbuch hierbei unterstützt werden.

Faltanleitung für ein Mini-Buch (1/2)

1.
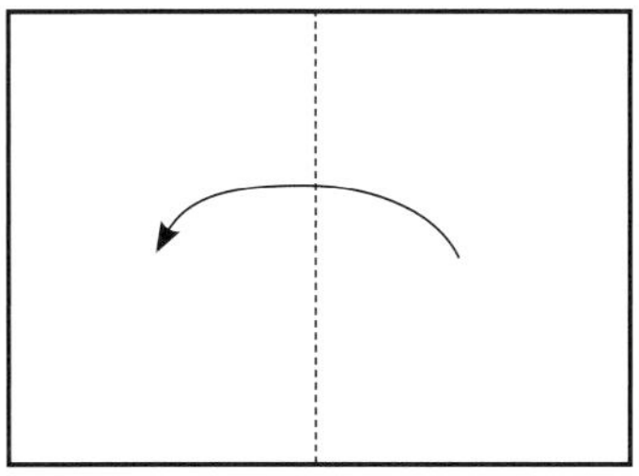

1. Lege das Blatt quer vor dich hin. Die bedruckte Seite ist unten. Falte das Blatt in der Mitte. Lege dazu die rechte Kante auf die linke.

2.
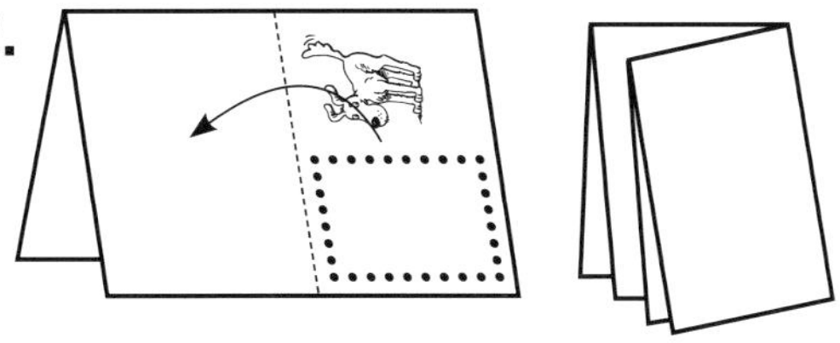

2. Drehe das Blatt ins Querformat. Die Öffnung zeigt nach unten. Falte das Blatt in der Mitte. Lege dazu die rechte Kante auf die linke.

3.
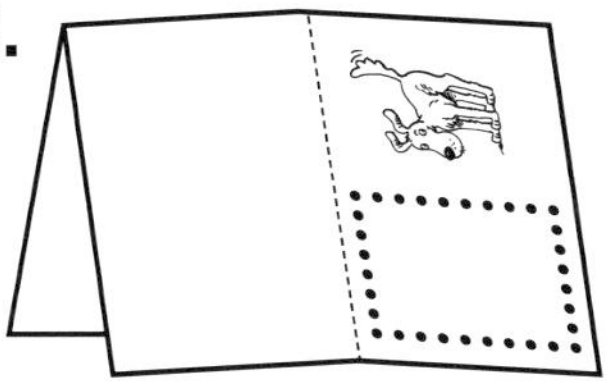

3. Falte das Blatt einmal wieder auf. Die Öffnung ist immer noch unten.

4.
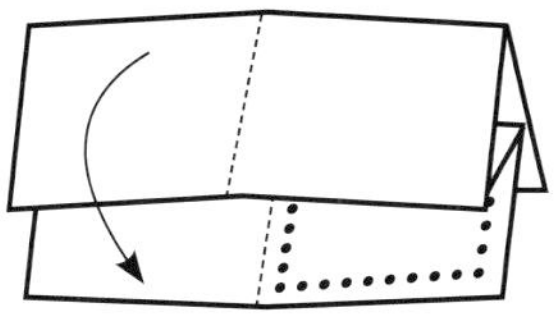

4. Falte die Oberkante auf die Unterkante. Klappe dann das Blatt wieder ganz auf. Lege das Blatt quer vor dich hin. Die bedruckte Seite ist unten.

5.

5. Falte die Oberkante auf die Unterkante. Falte die Felder zu einer Zickzacklinie.

6.
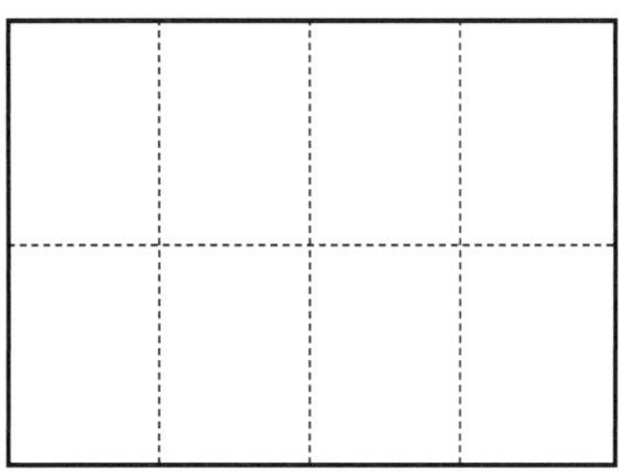

6. Falte das Blatt wieder auf. Es sind nun 8 senkrechte Felder zu sehen. Die bedruckte Seite ist wieder unten.

Faltanleitungen für ein Mini-Buch (2/2)

7.
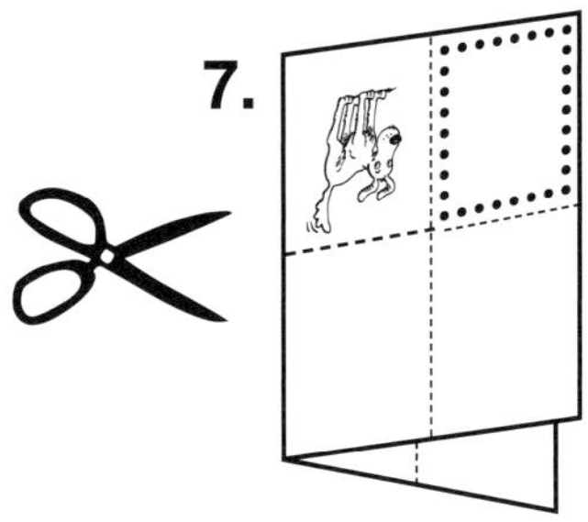

7. Falte den linken Seitenrand auf den rechten. Schneide die Falte in der Mitte entlang der gestrichelten Linie ein.

8.
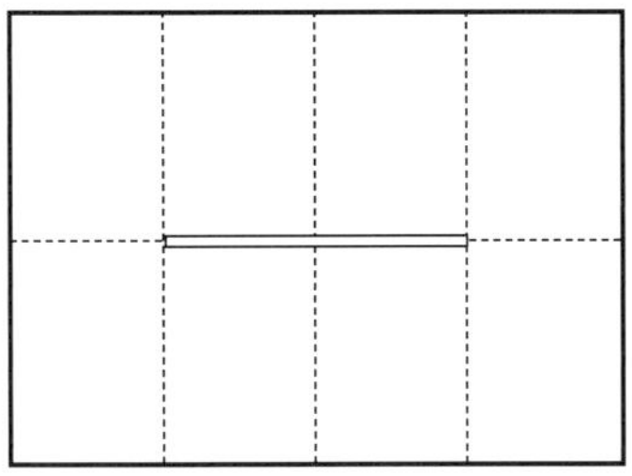

8. Falte das Blatt auf. Die bedruckte Seite ist unten. In der Mitte ist ein waagerechter Schlitz.

9.
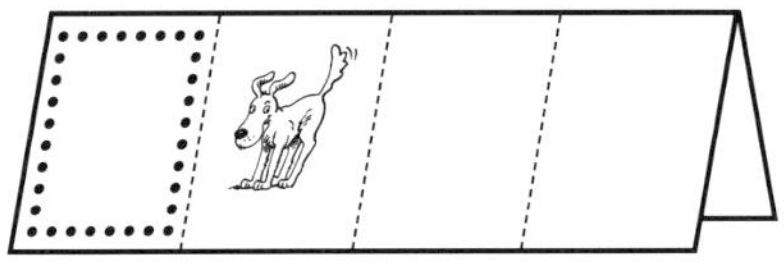

9. Falte die Oberkante auf die Unterkante.

10.
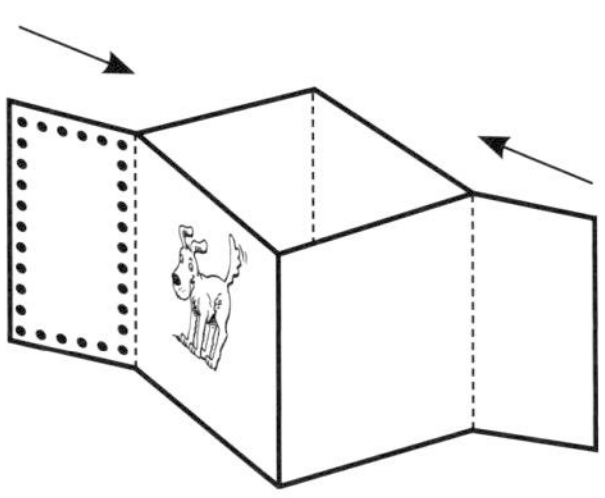

10. Schiebe den linken und den rechten Seitenrand gegeneinander. In der Mitte öffnet sich ein Viereck.

11.
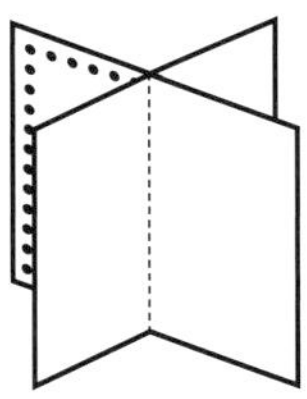

11. Schiebe die Seitenränder weiter zur Mitte. Die Oberkanten bilden nun ein Kreuz.

12.

12. Falte die Seiten so um, dass das Titelbild deines Büchleins obenauf liegt.

Nun kannst du dein Büchlein lesen und gestalten.

Viel Spaß!

Mini-Bücher

Nelly has got a big sister
and a big brother.
Her sister's name is Jenna
and her brother's name is Leo.
At the weekend,
Nelly's grandma Anni
and her grandpa Joseph
come to visit.
This is Nelly.
This is Nelly's mom.
Her name is Maja.
And this is Nelly's dad.
His name is Peter.

This is Nelly's family tree.
Fill in the names.
Nelly loves her family!
At the weekend,
Nelly's grandma Anni
and her grandpa Joseph
come to visit.
Draw a picture of your family.
Nelly's family
This is Nelly.

Nelly's family

Name:

1

This is Nelly.

2

This is Nelly's mom.
Her name is Maja.
And this is Nelly's dad.
His name is Peter.

3

Nelly has got a big sister
and a big brother.
Her sister's name is Jenna
and her brother's name is Leo.

4

At the weekend,
Nelly's grandma Anni
and her grandpa Joseph
come to visit.

5

Nelly loves her family!

6

This is Nelly's family tree.
Fill in the names.

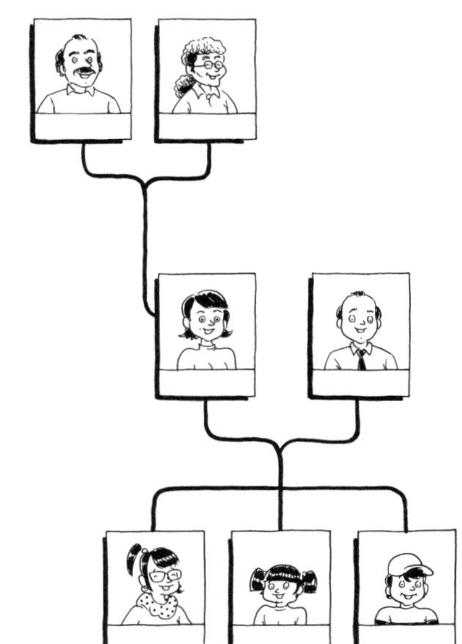

7

Draw a picture of your family.

8

 | ISBN 978-3-8346-4277-6

Autorin: Carolin Schirmer

Benny is crazy

Name:

This is Benny.
Benny is a bear.

"Benny, you are crazy!", says Berry, his brother.
But why?

Benny doesn't like honey.
And he doesn't like fish.
And he doesn't like strawberries.

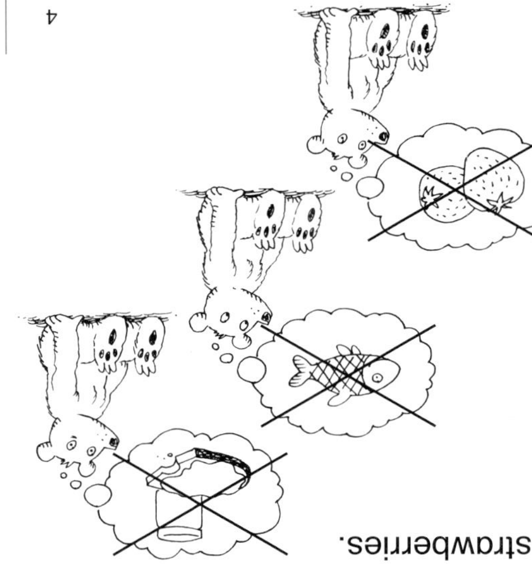

Benny doesn't like bananas.
And he doesn't like meat.
And he **hates** cheese!

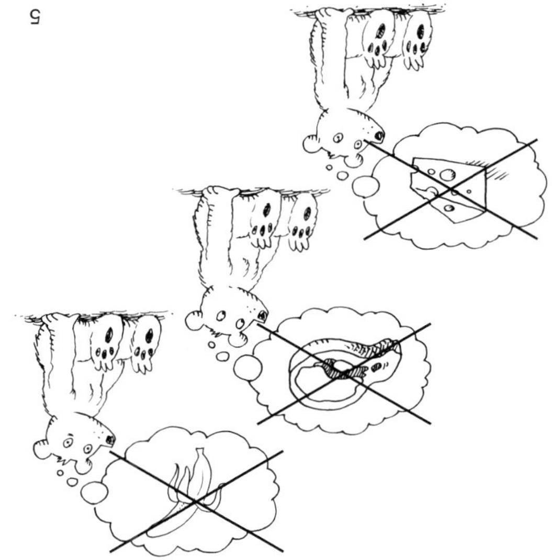

Benny likes ice cream!

True or false?
Tick the boxes.
true ✓ false ×

Benny likes cheese. .... ☐
Benny doesn't like ice cream. .... ☐
Benny likes bananas. .... ☐
Benny doesn't like meat. ...... ☐
Benny doesn't like honey. ..... ☐
Benny likes fish. .... ☐

What is your favourite food?
Draw a picture.

© Verlag an der Ruhr | Illustrationen: N. Höveler | ISBN 978-3-8346-4277-6
Autorin: Carolin Schirmer

Happy Halloween!

Name:

1

It's Halloween.
What costume do I want this year?

2

Maybe I want to be a witch.

3

Maybe I want to be a knight.

4

Oh! I have an idea!

5

This year, I want to be a dragon!

6

Write down the names next to the costumes.

 ....

 ....

 ....

7

Draw a picture of your favourite Halloween costume.

8

 | ISBN 978-3-8346-4277-6

Autorin: Carolin Schirmer

My Tuesday

Name:

Hi, I'm Nelly!
Today, it's Tuesday.
I get up at 7 o'clock.

Then I have breakfast
with my family.

At 8 o'clock, I go to school.
School is out at 12 o'clock.

After school, I eat lunch at home.
Later, I go swimming.

In the evening, I am tired.
I go to bed at 9 o'clock.

Write down Nelly's activities.

7 o'clock:
get up ....

8 o'clock:
....

12 o'clock:
....

after school:
....

9 o'clock:
....

What do you do on Tuesday?
Write down the correct time.

I get up at .... o'clock.

I eat breakfast at .... o'clock.

I go to school at .... o'clock.

School is out at .... o'clock.

I go to bed at .... o'clock.

Autorin: Carolin Schirmer

The number rhyme

1 2 9 3
10
7 5 8 6
4

Name:

One, two –
Let's go to the zoo.

Three, four –
Look at that paw.

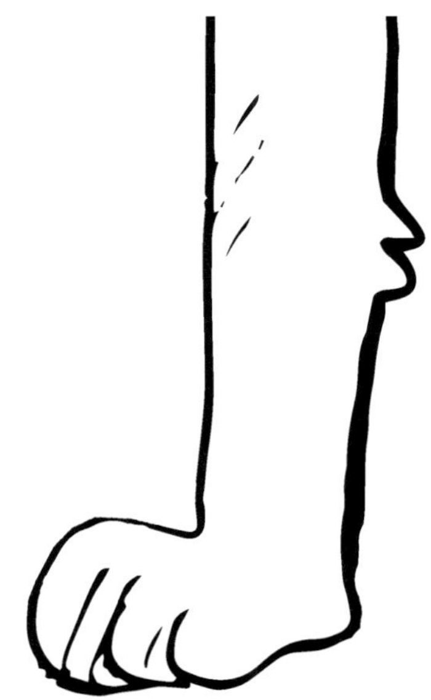

Five, six –
This is the lion Fix.

Seven, eight –
The lion is great!

Autorin: Carolin Schirmer

Nine, ten –
Can we go again?

Write down the number words.

1 one ....
2 ....
3 ....
4 ....
5 ....

Write down the number words.

6 six ....
7 ....
8 ....
9 ....
10 ....

What's missing?

Name:

This is a rabbit.
What's missing?
Oh, the ears are missing!

This is a bear.
What's missing?
Oh, the eyes are missing!

This is a monkey.
What's missing?
Oh, the mouth is missing!

This is a cat.
What's missing?
Oh, the nose is missing!

This is me.
What's missing?
Ears? Eyes? Mouth? Nose?
No! Nothing is missing!

Oh, look!

Here are the missing body parts! **Write down the names.**

 ....

 ....

 ....

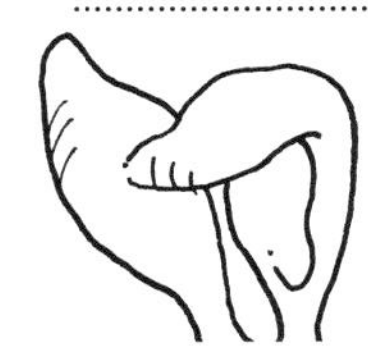 ....

Write your own "What's missing?" riddle and draw a picture.

This is a ....

What's missing?

The ....

Autorin: Carolin Schirmer

My favourite colour

Name:

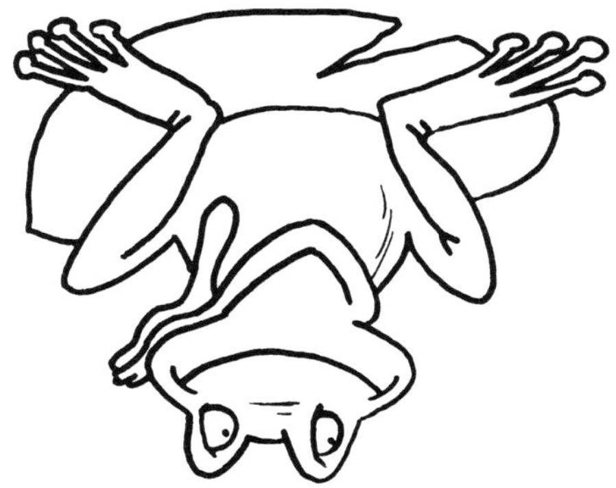

I'm a frog.
My favourite colour is green.

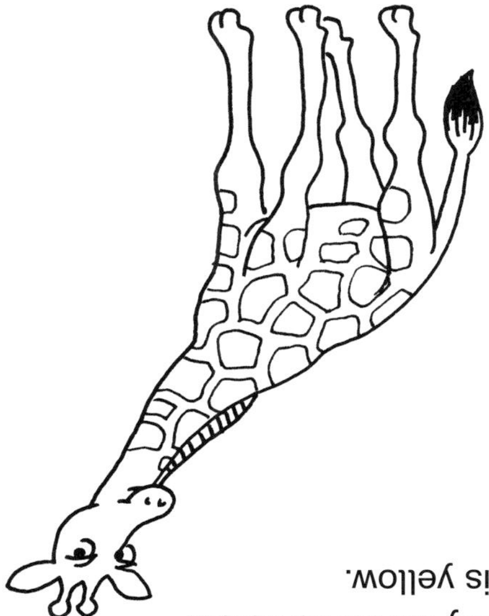

I'm a giraffe.
My favourite colour
is yellow.

I'm a dolphin.
My favourite colour is blue.

 | ISBN 978-3-8346-4277-6

I'm a ladybug.
My favourite colour is red.

Autorin: Carolin Schirmer

I'm a butterfly.
I love all colours!

Find a brown animal and draw a picture.

I'm a ....

Write down your name and your favourite colour.

My name is ....

My favourite colour is

....

Nice to meet you!

Name:

"Hello, my name is Janet.
What's your name?"

"Nice to meet you, Janet.
My name is Dennis.
What's your name?"

"Hello, Dennis.
My name is Mister Fuller.
What's your name?"

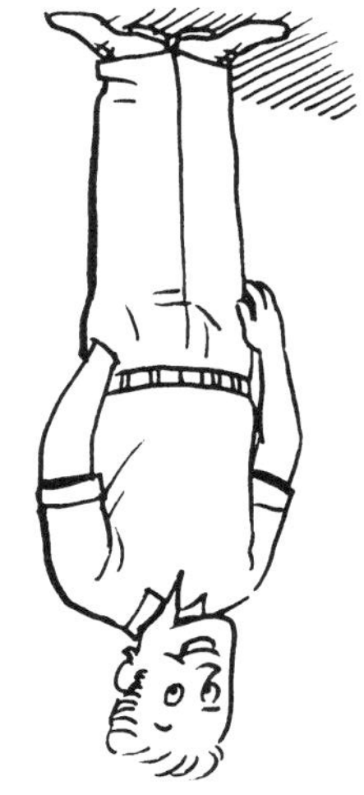

"Nice to meet you, Mister Fuller.
My name is Miss Pitt.
Oh! And what's your name?"

"Haha. This is my dog.
His name is Barry!"

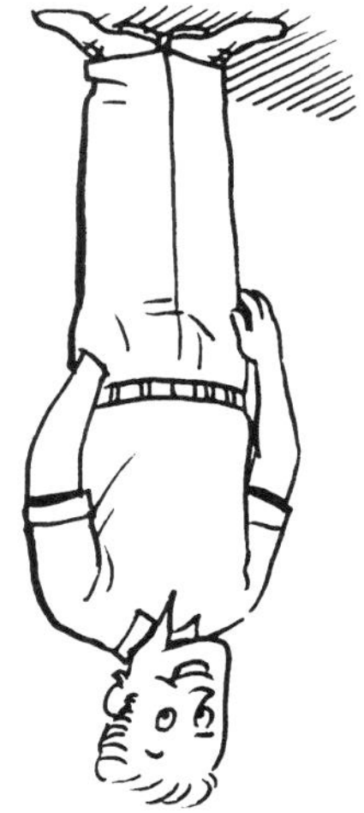

Write down the names under the pictures.

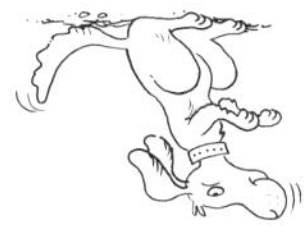

**Draw a picture of yourself.
Write down your name.**

Hello, my name is ....

....

Autorin: Carolin Schirmer

How are you?

Name: ....

1

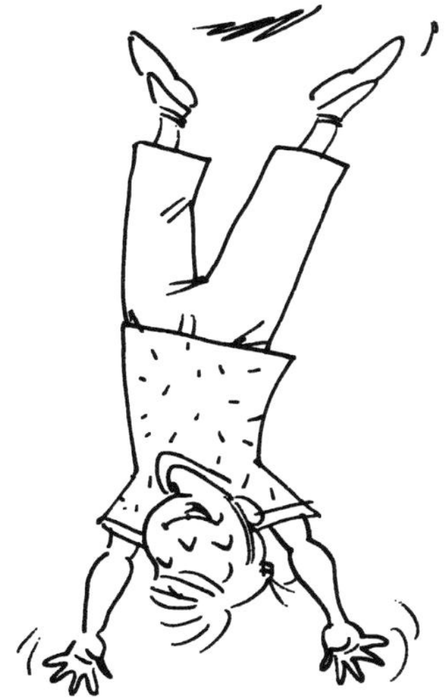

"How are you, Natalia?"
"I'm happy."

2

"How are you, Mike?"
"I'm angry!"

3

"How are you, Nina?"
"I'm sad."

4

"How are you, Artur?"
"I'm tired."

5

"And how are you, David and Alisha?"
"We are in love!"

6

Link the pictures with the feelings.

sad

angry

happy

in love

7

How are you today?
Tick the boxes.

- ☐ happy
- ☐ sad
- ☐ hungry
- ☐ tired
- ☐ angry
- ☐ in love
- ☐ thirsty
- ☐ surprised
- ☐ sick

8

© Verlag an der Ruhr | Illustrationen: N. Höveler | ISBN 978-3-8346-4277-6

Autorin: Carolin Schirmer

Who am I?

Name:

I don't go by car.
And I don't go by bike.

I don't go by bus.
And I don't go by train.

I don't go by ship.
And I don't go by boat.

Yes, I fly!
But I don't go by plane.

I am a bird!

What is it?

Write down the right word under the pictures.

....

....

How do you go to school?

Tick the box and draw a picture.

I …

- ☐ walk.
- ☐ go by bus.
- ☐ go by bike.
- ☐ go by car.

© Verlag an der Ruhr | Illustrationen: N. Höveler | ISBN 978-3-8346-4277-6

Autorin: Carolin Schirmer

Let's have breakfast

Name:

1

Next Monday, Tom's class wants to have breakfast. "Everyone has to bring something", says Miss Miller, the teacher.

2

"I can bring bread!", says Daniel.
"I can bring orange juice!", says Laura.

3

Hannah says: „I can bring butter!"
And Leo says:
„I can bring cheese!"

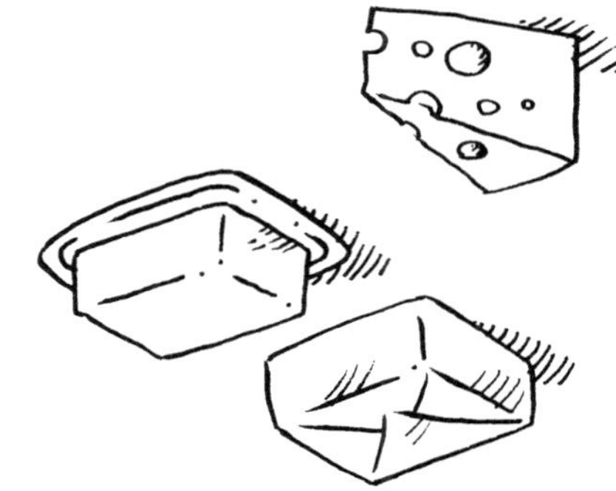

4

„I can bring jam!", says Lara.
„And I can bring eggs.
That's my favourite breakfast!", says Jan.

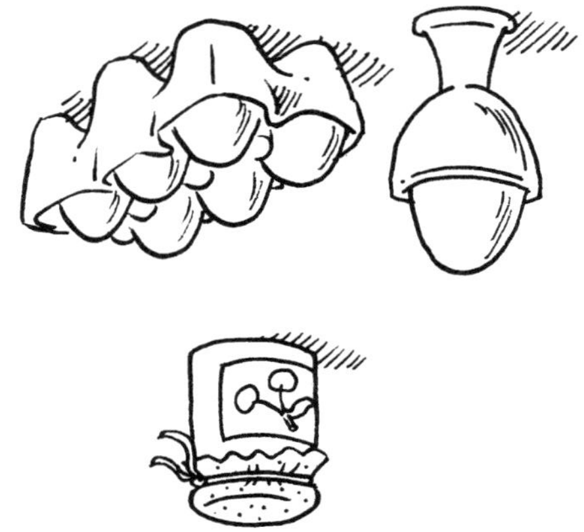

5

„And what can you bring, Tom?", asks Miss Miller.
Tom says: „I can bring fun!"
Everyone laughs.

6

What do the kids bring for breakfast?
Complete the list.

Daniel: ....

Laura: ....

Hannah: ....

Leo: ....

Lara: ....

Jan: ....

7

What's your favourite breakfast?
Write a sentence.
Then draw a picture.

My favourite breakfast is

....

8

Autorin: Carolin Schirmer

Bad weather

Name:

Jenny and Ben look outside.
It's cloudy, rainy and a bit windy.
Jenny and Ben are sad.

The next day, it's rainy and cold.
Jenny and Ben get a postcard
from their friend Paul.

„Dear Jenny, dear Ben!
Hello from Mallorca. The
weather is hot and sunny.
See you soon! Paul."

„Okay, let's go outside!", says
Ben.
„But Ben! It's cold and rainy!",
says Jenny.

„But we have got capes and
boots!", says Ben.
„Great idea!"

Can you find all 6 weather
words in the story?
Write them down.

cloudy, ...

....

....

....

....

What's the weather like today?

Tick the boxes and draw a picture.

☐ cold	☐ cloudy
☐ rainy	☐ sunny
☐ foggy	☐ snowy
☐ warm	☐ hot

Greg's week

Name:

1

This is Greg.
Greg has a very busy week.
On Monday, he plays tennis.

2

On Tuesday and on Wednesday, Greg goes dancing.

3

On Thursday, Greg plays the guitar.

4

And on Friday, Greg rides a bike.

5

On Saturday, Greg plays video games.

6

... And on Sunday?
Draw a picture of Greg's Sunday activity.

7

Write down the 7 days of the week.
You can use different colours.

Monday ....

....

....

....

....

....

8

Autorin: Carolin Schirmer

New clothes for Jenna

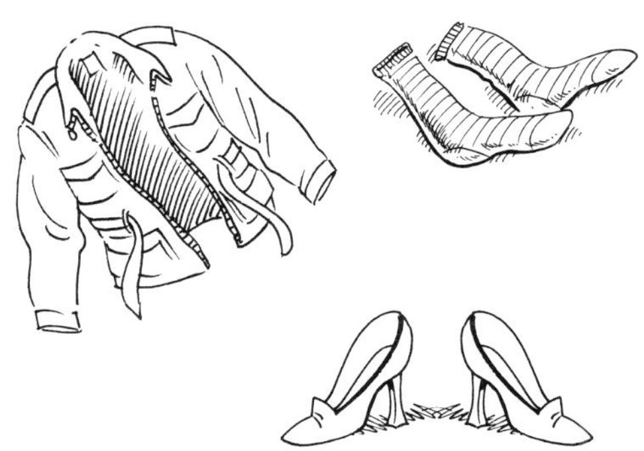

Name:

Jenna wants to go shopping.
She needs new clothes.

“I need new jeans.
And I need a new jacket.”

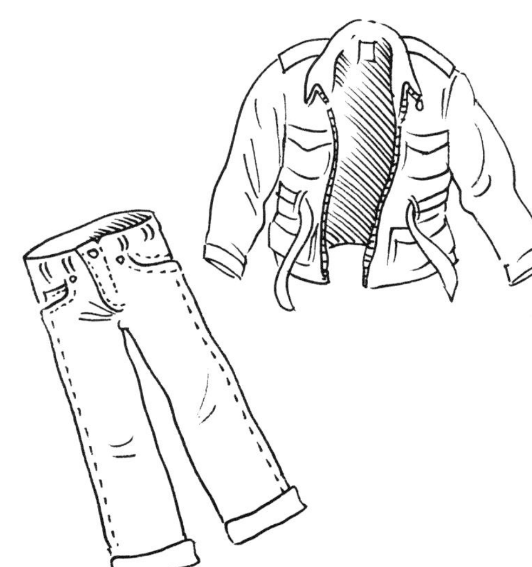

„I need a new dress.
And I need t-shirts for summer.“

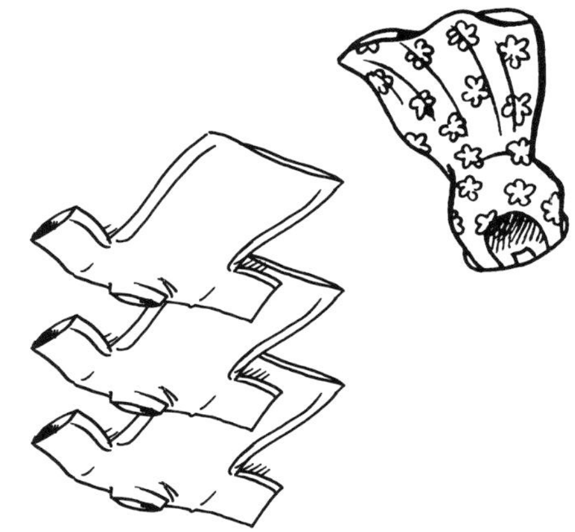

„I need new socks.
Oh, and of couse,I need
new shoes!“

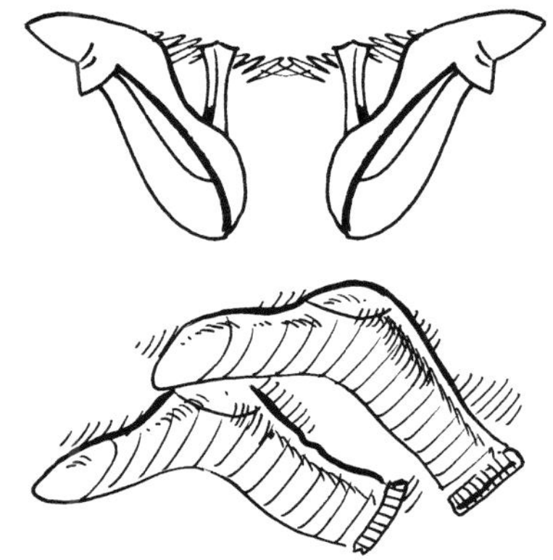

Jenna looks at her shopping list.
„I think I need a new wardrobe!“

What’s on Jenna’s
shopping list?

Tick the boxes.

- ☐ jeans
- ☐ dress
- ☐ skirt
- ☐ shoes
- ☐ pullover

Do you need new clothes, too?

Write down sentences and draw pictures.

I need new ……………………………………

……………………………………

Autorin: Carolin Schirmer

Freddy's year

Name:

In school, Freddy's class talks about their plans for next year. Freddy has got lots of ideas!

"In spring, I make a picnic
with my family.
We eat fruits and drink ice tea."

"In summer, I go swimming
at the beach!
And I eat lots of ice cream."

"In autumn, I go walking
in the forest.
And I often ride a bike
with my friends."

"In winter, I build a snowman
with my sister.
And then, it's Christmas!
Winter is my favourite season!"

Link Freddy's acitivities and the seasons.

winter

summer

autumn

spring

What's your favourite season?

My favourite season is ....

....

What do you do then?

Draw a picture.

Autorin: Carolin Schirmer

Merry Christmas

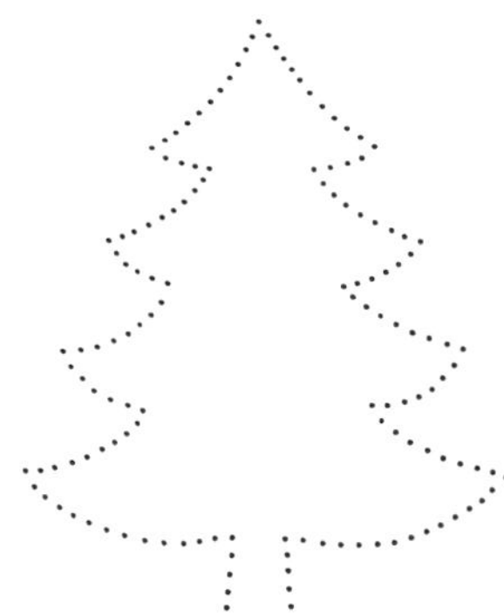

Name:

It's Christmas! Finally!
Mia and Luke are very excited.

In the morning, Mia and Luke
decorate the Christmas tree.

In the afternoon, Mia's and
Luke's grandmas and grandpas
come to visit.
They drink coffee, hot chocolate
and eat cookies.

In the evening, the family
sings Christmas songs.
Luke plays the piano.

Then Mia and Luke want to see
their presents!
But what's that?
Bobby, the dog, eats the
wrapping!
The family laughs.

What do Mia and Luke do
on Christmas?

Tick the correct answers.

- ☐ sing Christmas songs
- ☐ visit their uncles and aunts
- ☐ build a snowman
- ☐ decorate the Christmas tree
- ☐ eat cookies
- ☐ play the guitar

What do you wish for Christmas?

Write down sentences and draw pictures.

....

....

Autorin: Carolin Schirmer

Oh no, Tiffy!

Name:

Paul is happy.
He has got a new pet: a little dog, Tiffy.
Paul shows Tiffy the house.

"Look, Tiffy. This is our living room. Here is the TV and …"
Tiffy jumps on the sofa.
"Oh, no, Tiffy! Not on the sofa!"

"Look, Tiffy. This is our bathroom.
Here is a shower and …"
Tiffy jumps on the toilet.
"Oh no, Tiffy! Not on the toilet!"

© Verlag an der Ruhr | Illustrationen: N. Höveler | ISBN 978-3-8346-4277-6

"Look, Tiffy. This is our kitchen.
There is a fridge and …"
Tiffy jumps on a chair.
"Oh no, Tiffy! Not on the chair!"

Autorin: Carolin Schirmer

"Look, Tiffy. This is my bedroom.
Here is my bed."
Tiffy looks at Paul.
"Haha, Tiffy. Yes, you can jump on my bed! Let's play!"

Which rooms does Paul show Tiffy?

Write down the names.

....

....

....

....

Draw a picture of a room in your home.

Nicky can do it better

Name:

1

This is Nicky, the mouse.
And this is Matt, the sloth.
They are best friends.

2

Nicky can run faster than Matt.
“That’s okay”, says Matt.

3

Nicky can jump higher than Matt.
„That’s okay”, says Matt.

4

Nicky can swim better than Matt.
„That’s okay”, says Matt.

5

But what can Matt do better than Nicky?
„I can sleep longer!”

6

Which sentence is correct?

Tick the right boxes.

☐ Nicky can run faster than Matt.

☐ Nicky can sleep longer than Matt.

☐ Matt can swim better than Nicky.

☐ Nicky can jump higher than Matt.

7

What can you do better than your friends?

Write it down or draw a picture.

8

Autorin: Carolin Schirmer

Let's go to school

Name:

Hello, I'm Nelly.
I want to show you my way to school.

At first, I go left.
Then I go straight on.

There is a traffic light.
I wait for the green light.
Then I cross the street.

I go straight on.
At the end of the street, I turn right.

Look, there is my school!

Draw Nelly's way to her school.

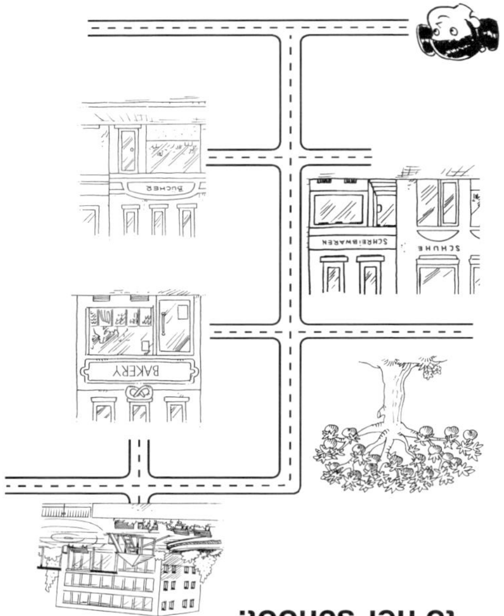

Write down your way to school/ to your best friend/ to your sports club ...
You can use these words:
go straight on, turn left, turn right, cross the street

....

....

....

....

Autorin: Carolin Schirmer

Busy day

Name:

1

Today is a busy day for
Nelly's family.
Nelly is cleaning the bathroom.

2

Nelly's dad is tidying up his
room.

3

Jenna is doing the laundry.

4

Nelly's mum is cooking.

5

And Leo?
He is busy, too. Leo is playing
computer games …

6

Link the persons and their activities.

cleaning the bathroom

doing the laundry

cooking

tidying up his room

7

What do you do on a busy day? Tidying up your room? Cleaning? Cooking?

Write it down or draw a picture.

8

Opposites

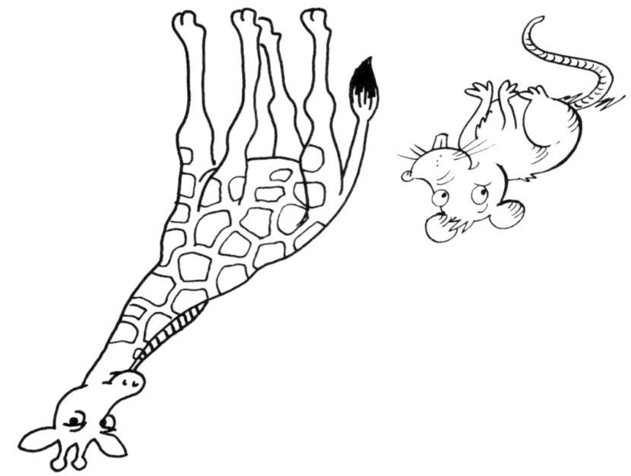

Name:

The hippo looks at the giraffe.
It says: "I am fat. You are thin."

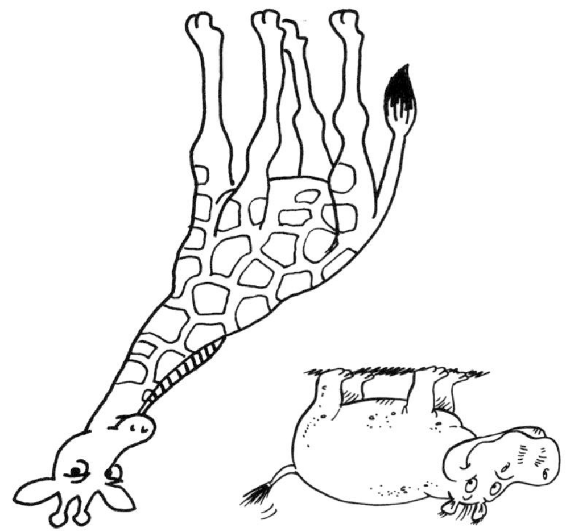

The giraffe looks at the mouse.
It says: "I am big.
You are small."

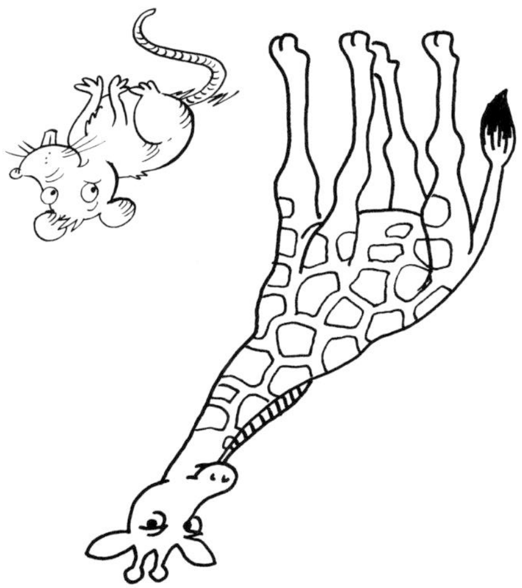

The mouse looks at the turtle.
It says: "I am fast.
You are slow."

The turtle looks at the rabbit.
It says: "I am old.
You are young."

The elephant looks around.
He says: "That's great!
We are all different. But we
are all happy!"

Link the opposites.

fat ☐	☐ small
old ☐	☐ thin
fast ☐	☐ young
big ☐	☐ slow

Draw a picture of 2 opposites, for example happy – sad, hot – cold, long – short …

© Verlag an der Ruhr | Illustrationen: N. Höveler | ISBN 978-3-8346-4277-6

Autorin: Carolin Schirmer

Lilly's birthday

Name:

1

Today is Lilly's birthday.

2

Lilly gets a big birthday cake and lots of presents.

3

At school, the class sings „Happy bithday" for Lilly.
„How old are you now, Lilly?",
asks Mister Baker, the teacher.
„I am 9 years old", says Lilly.

4

Then Lilly's best friends come for her birthday party.
They play funny games.

5

In the evening, Lilly is very happy.
"This was the best day ever!"

6

True or false?
Tick the boxes.
true ✓ false ×

Today is Emma's birthday...... ☐

Lilly gets a big birthday bread. .... ☐

The class sings „Happy birthday". .... ☐

Lilly is 9 years old. .... ☐

In the evening, Lilly is very sad. .... ☐.

7

What was your best birthday present? **Draw a picture.**

8

Fruit rhyme

Name:

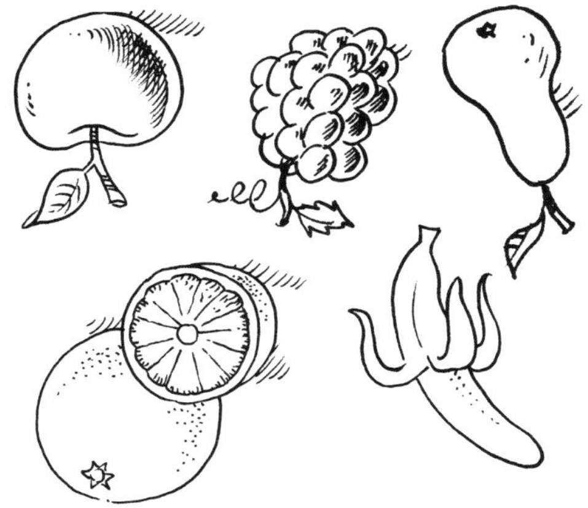

I like oranges.
Oranges are great!

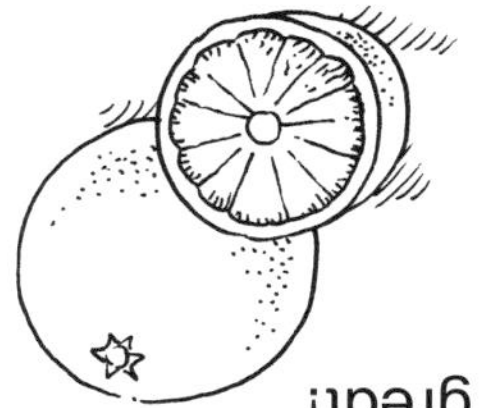

But I don't like bananas.
They are what I hate.

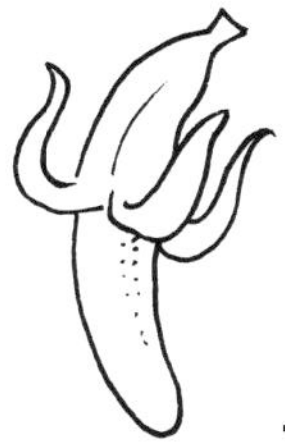

I don't like grapes a lot.
Grapes are just okay.

But I really like green apples.
I eat them every day.

I like pears.
Pears are really cool!

Oh, and I like strawberries.
I eat them at my school.

There are fruits I like
and there are fruits I hate.
But do you know what I like
best?

A big, big chocolate cake!

Write down the fruit names.

 ....

 ....

 ....

 ....

 ....

Which fruits do you like?
Write them down and draw a picture.

I like ....

....

Autorin: Carolin Schirmer

At the bakery

Name:

„Good morning, Miss Fisher.
Can I help you?"

„Yes, please.
3 rolls, 2 croissants and a
piece of cake, please.
How much is it?"

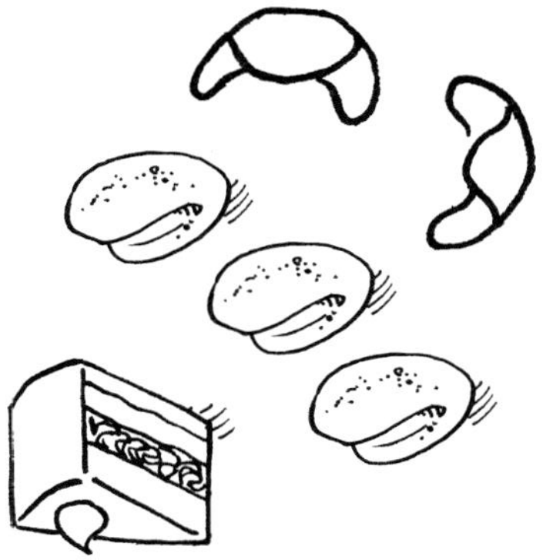

"It's 3 pounds."
"Okay, fine. Here you are."
"Thank you. Have a nice day."
"You, too. Good bye!"

"Oh no! My rolls! My croissants!
My piece of cake!"

"Okay …
3 rolls, 2 croissants and
a piece of cake, please …
again."

What does Miss Fisher buy
at the bakery?

Tick the right boxes.

☐ 3 rolls

☐ 1 bread

☐ 2 croissants

☐ 3 cookies

☐ a piece of cake

What do you want to buy
at the bakery?

Write it down and draw a picture.

……………………………, please.

A toy for Anna

Name: ....

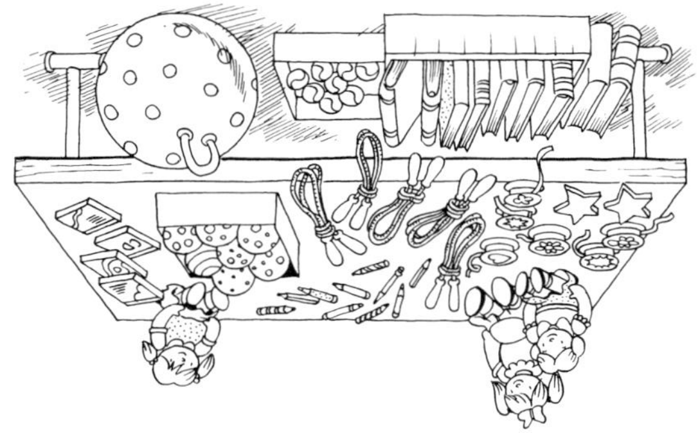

1

"Hey, Anna! Let's buy a toy for you", says Anna's dad.
"Great idea!"

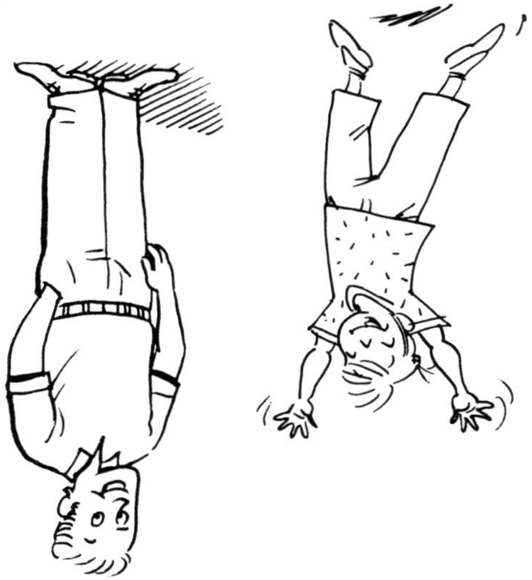

2

"Oh, look, Anna: a doll!
Do you want to have the doll?"
"No, I don't.
I don't like dolls."

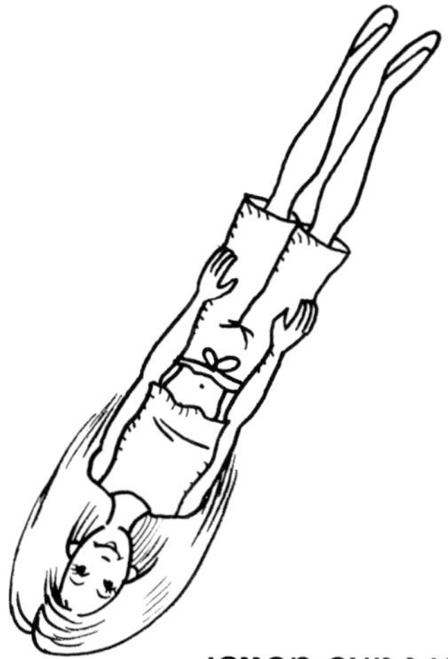

3

"Oh, look, Anna: a teddy bear!
Do you want to have
the teddy bear?"
"No, I don't.
I don't like teddy bears."

4

"Oh, look, Anna: a skipping
rope! Do you want to have
the skipping rope?"
"No, I don't.
I don't like skipping ropes."

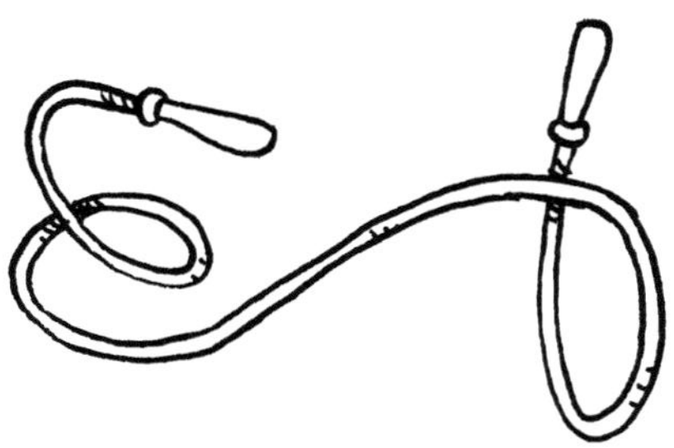

5

"Oh, Anna. You don't like dolls.
You don't like teddy bears.
You don't like skipping ropes.
What do you like?"
"I like toy cars!"

6

Anna likes toy cars.
What toys does Anna **not** like?

Tick the right boxes.

☐ skateboards

☐ dolls

☐ skipping ropes

☐ footballs

☐ bikes

☐ teddy bears

7

What's your favourite toy?

Write the name and draw a picture.

....

....

8

© Verlag an der Ruhr | Illustrationen: N. Höveler | ISBN 978-3-8346-4277-6

Autorin: Carolin Schirmer

Name:

I spy with my little eye …

1

Sally and Nick are at home.
It's boring.
"Let's play *I spy with my little eye!*", says Sally.

2

Nick says: "I spy with my little eye something **green**."
Sally looks around
"Oh! My t-shirt!"
"Yes, that's right!", says Nick.

3

Sally says: "I spy with my little eye something **brown**."
Nick looks around.
"The desk? Oh, or the chair?"
"No", laughs Sally.
"The teddy!"
"Yes, that's right!"

4

Nick says: "I spy with my little eye something **blue**."
Sally looks around.
"Your bag? My jeans? Your shoes? The lamp?", asks Sally.
"No! The poster!", says Nick.

5

Sally is angry.
"The poster is red and yellow and orange and black and…"
"Yes. And it's blue", Nick laughs.

6

The poster in the story has lots of colours.
What does it look like?

Draw a picture of the poster.

7

Look around. What do you spy with your little eye?

Write sentences.

I spy with my little eye ....

something ....

It's ....

I spy with my little eye ....

something ....

It's ....

8

Name:

Phil goes to school

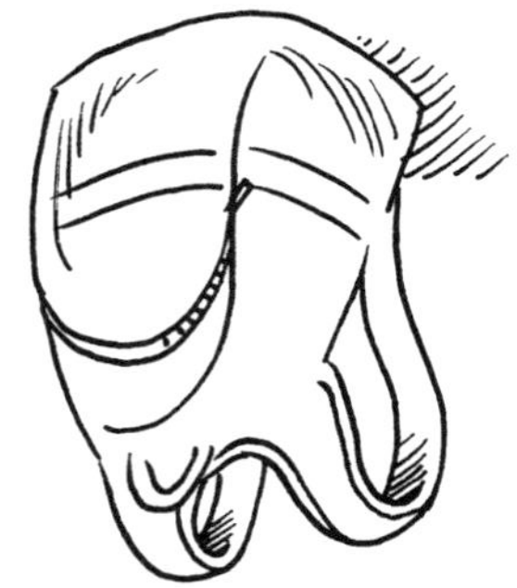

In the morning, Phil packs
his school bag.

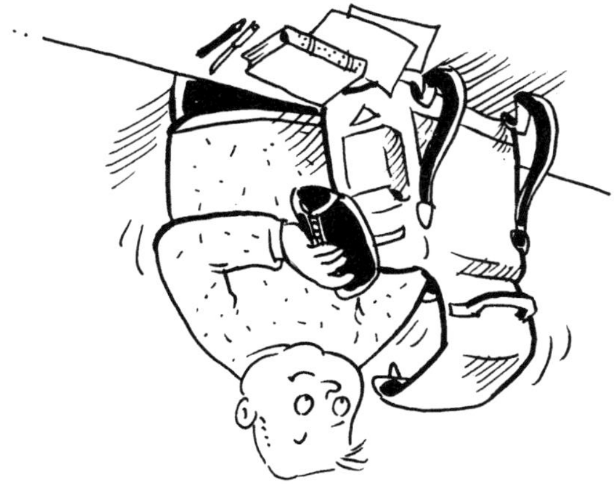

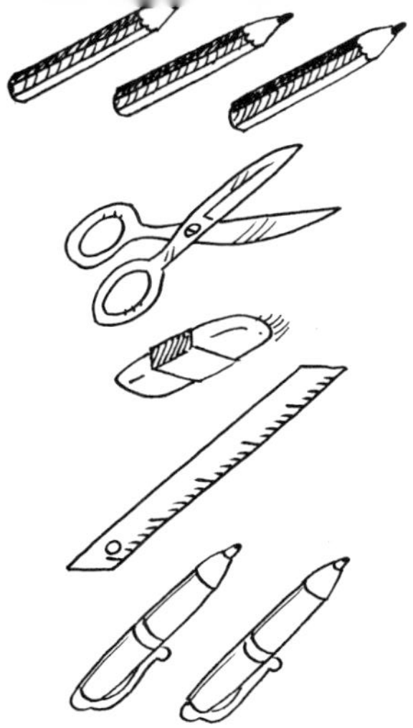

He packs his pencil case.
In the pencil case, there are 2
pens, a ruler, a rubber, scissors
and coloured pencils.

Then, Phil packs his books
and his folders.
Ready?
"Oh, no, my lunchbox!"

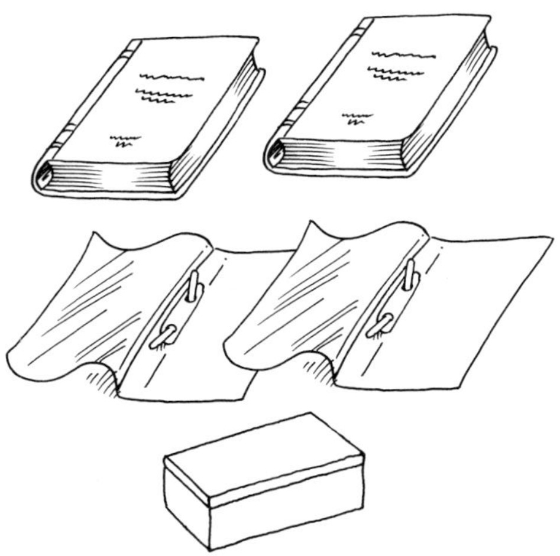

"Bye, mum! Bye, dad!"
Phil wants to go to the bus stop.

"Phil, where are you going?
Today is Sunday – no school!",
Phil's mum says.

What's in Phil's school bag?

Tick the right boxes.

☐ pencil case

☐ sharpener

☐ folders

☐ scissors

☐ milk

☐ 5 pens

☐ lunchbox

What's in your school bag?

Draw pictures.

ISBN 978-3-8346-4277-6

Autorin: Carolin Schirmer

Pets

Name:

1

Class 4c talks about their pets.
"I have got a dog.
His name is Rocky!", says Julia.

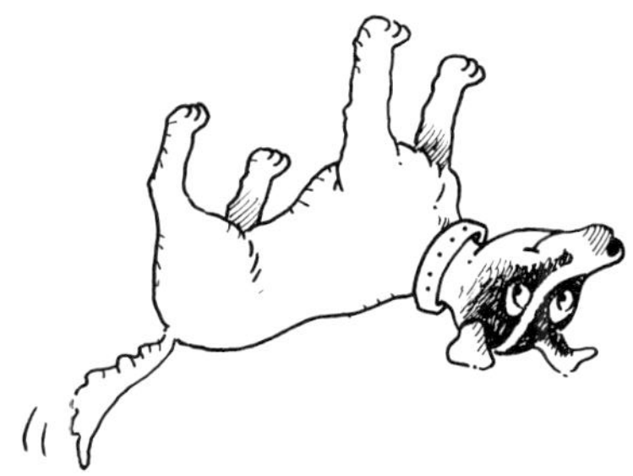

2

Martin says: "I have got a rabbit and a mouse. Their names are Fred and Frieda. They are best friends!"

3

Susie has got a cat: Jerry.
And Milo has got a fish.
"What's his name?", asks Miss Ring, the teacher.
"His name is Fish", laughs Milo.

4

"And you, Miss Ring?", asks Nela.
Miss Ring says: "I have got 5 cows, 4 horses, 8 ducks, 10 pigs …"

5

The class is surprised:
So many pets?
Miss Ring laughs: "I live on a farm!"

6

Link the child and its pet.

Julia ☐	☐ dog
Martin ☐	☐ cat
Susie ☐	☐ fish
Milo ☐	☐ mouse and rabbit

7

Draw a picture of your favourite pet.

8

Name:

Suri in London

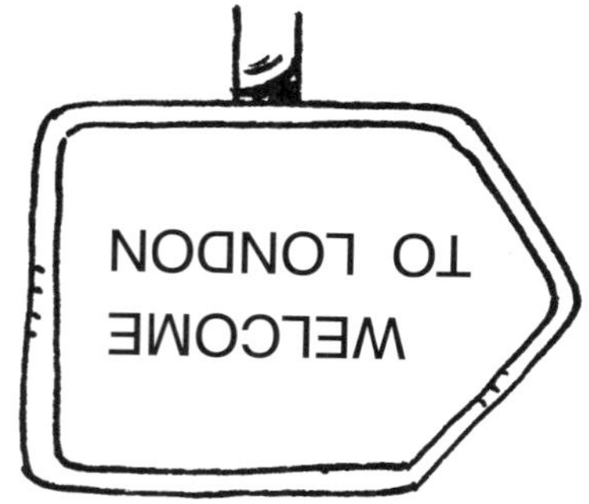

Suri is in London with her family.

Suri visits Buckingham Palace.
The Queen lives here.
But Suri can't see the Queen.
Too bad!

Then Suri takes the London underground. That's cool! But Suri also likes the red buses.

Suri takes a picture next to a phone box.

In the evening, Suri tells her dad: "London is great!! Tomorrow, I want to visit Big Ben, the Tower Bridge, and …ch-puuuu …. ch-puuuu …." Ooops. Suri was too tired …

Suri can't see the Queen.

Draw a picture of the Queen.

This is the Union Jack, the flag of Great Britain.

Look for the correct colours and colour the flag.

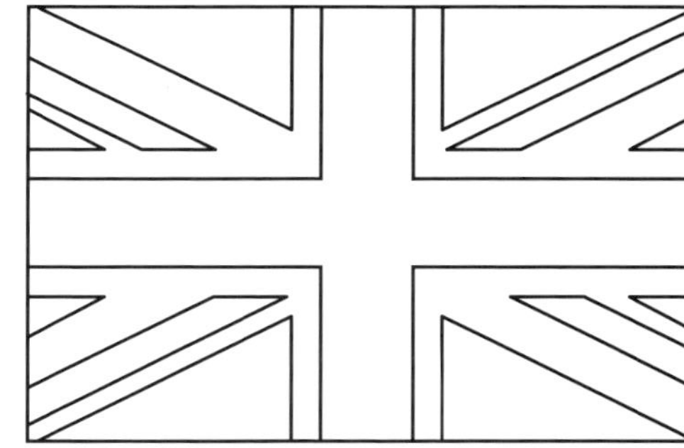

 ISBN 978-3-8346-4277-6

Autorin: Carolin Schirmer

The Valentine's card

Name:

Felix loves Linda.
Linda is cool and funny and clever.
Linda is the best!

Tomorrow, it's Valentine's day.
Felix writes a Valentine's card for Linda.

"Dear Linda!
I like you a lot. Do you want to go to the cinema with me?
Love, Felix."

It's Valentine's day!
Felix puts his Valentine's card into Linda's school bag.

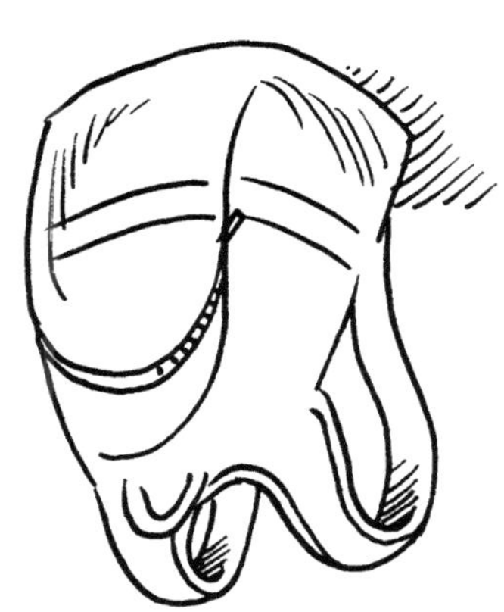

Linda reads the Valentine's card.
She smiles.
"Let's go to the cinema!"
Felix is happy.

Which sentence is correct?
Tick the right boxes.

- ☐ Felix loves Linda.
- ☐ Felix wants to go to the zoo with Linda.
- ☐ Linda cries.
- ☐ Felix writes a Valentine's card for Linda.
- ☐ Felix puts the Valentine's card into Linda's lunchbox.

Draw a picture of Linda and Felix at the cinema.

4

5

Autorin: Carolin Schirmer

6

7

3

2

1

Name: ....

8